Stories Jesus Told

Other titles by Avril Rowlands

All the Tales From the Ark

The Animals' Caravan: The Journey Begins

Look out for this symbol *. You will find these stories in this first book of the series.

The Animals' Caravan

Stories Jesus Told

A Journey through the Bible
with Caravan Bear and friends

Avril Rowlands

Illustrated by Kay Widdowson

LION
CHILDREN'S

To Nick Wright
With my love and thanks for your friendship and help   A. R.

Published by Lion Children's Books
an imprint of
Lion Hudson Limited
Wilkinson House, Jordan Hill Business Park,
Banbury Road, Oxford OX2 8DR, England
www.lionhudson.com/lionchildrens

ISBN 978 0 7459 7757 7

e-ISBN 978 0 7459 7804 8

First edition 2018

A catalogue record for this book is available from the British Library

Printed and bound in the UK, May 2018, LH26

Contents

A Cold Start

"Close the door!" said Hector the horse angrily as Caravan Bear opened his stable door, letting in a wave of cold air.

"It's not that bad," said Caravan Bear.

"Yes, it is," said Hector. "I wouldn't mind if it were winter, but it's supposed to be spring."

"It *is* spring – and time we were off on our travels!"

Every spring Caravan Bear would hitch Hector up to the caravan and, with Whitby the dog, they would set off in search of new adventures. Every autumn they would return to the paddock and the small patch of garden where they would stay until it was spring again.

"You go, then. I'm staying here in my nice warm stable."

Caravan Bear went up to Hector and stroked his nose. "Now, what is all this?" he asked. "You love going away."

"Yes, but not when it's cold and wet. Anyway, you said you had work to do on the caravan."

"I've done it. Well, most of it."

"Why can't we go in a week or two when the weather's better?"

"You know we can't. Christopher Rabbit is expecting us."

"Can't he wait?"

"It's his birthday."

Whitby ran in, her tail waving behind her.

"Come on, Hector – time we were off!"

Hector began nibbling some hay.

"He doesn't want to go," Caravan Bear explained.

"Yet. I want to go but not yet," Hector retorted. "I'll go when it's warmer."

"We can't let Christopher Rabbit down," Whitby cried. "It's…

"… his birthday," Hector finished. "I know. What's so important about Christopher Rabbit's birthday?"

"It's when we first met him. Don't you remember?

He was standing in the road, holding this big book in his hand, and…"

"… and I nearly ran him down, silly animal."

"But then he came with us on our travels and read us those wonderful stories from the Bible."

"And we had a lovely summer," Caravan Bear went on. "You said it had been the best summer you'd ever had."

"All those adventures…" Whitby added.

"Yes, like getting stuck in the rain," Hector grumbled, not wanting to be convinced.

"Oh, don't be such a misery," said Whitby.

"Well, we can't let Christopher Rabbit down, so we're going just as soon as I've finished a few jobs and packed the caravan," said Caravan Bear. "And I'd better go now or we'll be late." He smiled at Hector. "If it's cold, you can wear your warm new coat – the one we gave you for Christmas. Very smart you'll look, too!"

With that, Caravan Bear and Whitby left the stable.

"Shut that door!" Hector called after them, but he wasn't really angry. He was remembering how much fun they all had last year. He was also thinking how good he would look in his new coat.

"Where are we going first?" asked Whitby, prancing around Caravan Bear as they went over to the caravan. It was standing looking very fine in its bright new coat of red paint and its brilliant yellow wheels.

"Here, there, wherever the fancy takes us," said Caravan Bear – as he always did at the start of their adventures.

He looked proudly at his handiwork and smiled happily.

Christopher Rabbit looked anxiously out of the window; then, for the tenth time, went over to the door, opened it, looked up and down the street, sniffed the air, and closed the door again. Would they come or wouldn't they? They had said they would come on his birthday and today was his birthday, but he hadn't heard anything from them – and the weather wasn't really ideal for starting out on holiday. It was grey and cold and beginning to rain.

All day long there had been a procession of his friends from the village, wishing him a happy birthday, bringing him presents, hoping he would have a good trip, and asking him when he would be going.

"Soon," he had said. "I'll be off soon." But as the day wore on, he became less sure.

His small bag that he had packed two days before sat forlornly by the front door. On top of it was the Bible.

Now that had been a strange thing, Christopher Rabbit remembered.

It was on his birthday last year that he had run

out of his house, upset because no one had come to his birthday party and no one had given him any presents or cards. He smiled as he remembered that no one had come because he had forgotten to post any invitations. But at the time he thought he hadn't any friends at all. So he had put on his scarf, rushed out of the house and fallen over a brightly wrapped parcel that had been left in the road outside his front gate. The handwritten label said CHRISTOPHER RABBIT in large letters.

Inside was a book. A big book with the words THE BIBLE on the cover. When he opened it, he found the handwritten words "Read Me" on the first page.

Then a caravan had come hurtling down the road toward him. He had been sure he would be run over. But the caravan stopped just in time and Caravan Bear, Whitby, and Hector had invited him in. A spring and summer of wonderful adventures had followed.

He had been very sad to leave them and go home at the end of the holiday. He thought the winter would be very long and very lonely without his new friends. But it hadn't. Surrounded by friendly neighbours, the time had soon passed.

He had helped Henry the beaver and his family when the dam they built across their stream overflowed and their home had been flooded; he had dug the dormouse out of a snowdrift; he had searched for fresh nuts when Susie the squirrel's hoard had been stolen; and in the evenings he would often find Min, the cat who lived next door, curled up on his hearthrug in front of a warm fire. In fact, he had been so busy he had not even had time to open his Bible, let alone read the stories inside.

Perhaps he would have time now, he thought, once they were all off on their travels.

If they were off on their travels.

… If the brightly painted caravan came bouncing down the road pulled by Hector, going too fast as usual, with Caravan Bear and Whitby sitting on the steps, holding on tightly to the sides.

… If they hadn't forgotten him…

For the eleventh time, Christopher Rabbit opened his front door, went outside, and peered up and down the street. It was just beginning to get dark. They wouldn't come now.

But then he heard a loud clip, clop, clip, clop and saw two bobbing lights racing toward him. Hector pulled up sharply and Caravan Bear and Whitby tumbled down the steps.

"Sorry we're late," said Caravan Bear breathlessly.

"It was Hector's fault," said Whitby.

"No, it wasn't," said Hector.

"Yes, it was. You didn't want to come."

"Of course I wanted to come. I just wasn't sure about the weather. But I'm nice and warm now in my new coat." He looked at Christopher Rabbit expectantly.

"It's a very smart coat," Christopher Rabbit said hurriedly.

"Yes, it is, isn't it?" Hector turned to Whitby. "Why do you always blame me?"

"Because it's always your fault," Whitby replied.

Christopher Rabbit looked from one to the other and a slow smile spread across his face.

"It's so good to see you all," he said. "I'll just get my bag."

"And the Bible," Caravan Bear called after him as he ran back up the path.

"We want some more stories," called Whitby.

"Especially ones with horses in them," Hector added.

"Where are we going?" Christopher Rabbit asked when he had collected his bag and the Bible, climbed the steps, and sat down between Caravan Bear and Whitby.

"Oh, here…" Caravan Bear began.

"… and there…" said Whitby.

"WHEREVER THE FANCY TAKES US!" shouted Hector as, with a jerk, he tossed his mane, gave a loud neigh, and set off up the street at a lively pace.

"Slow down, Hector!" Caravan Bear shouted, but Hector only snorted and went faster than ever.

Christopher Rabbit smiled again, feeling very happy. They were on their way!

2

No Room at the Inn

They kept up a good pace as the sky darkened and the rain turned to sleet. Then Hector suddenly stopped.

"Which way?" he asked.

They had arrived at a crossroads. They could turn left, or right, or take the smaller track straight ahead.

"Left," said Caravan Bear.

"Right," said Whitby at the same time.

"What do you think, Hector?" asked Christopher Rabbit.

Hector shrugged. "Don't ask me," he said. "I'm only the driver."

"What do you think, Christopher Rabbit?" asked Whitby.

Christopher Rabbit looked left, then right, then straight ahead.

"Well," he said. "Ahead looks a bit more interesting, although it's hard to see properly as it's getting dark."

"Ahead it is, then," Hector snorted and set off.

At first it seemed a good road to have taken, but then it grew narrower and narrower, and Caravan Bear winced as the sides of the caravan were scratched with overhanging brambles. The surface of the road grew worse, with great holes and deep ruts on either side, and the caravan bounced up and down.

"I feel sick," said Whitby.

"I'm sorry," said Christopher Rabbit. "It wasn't a very good choice."

"Can't we turn around?" asked Whitby.

"There's no opening to turn into," said Caravan Bear.

At that moment there was a grinding sound, and a crack – and the caravan fell down on one side! Hector stopped with a jerk while Christopher Rabbit, Whitby, and Caravan Bear were thrown off the steps into the muddy road.

"What's happened?" Hector asked in a dazed voice.

Caravan Bear walked around the caravan. "A wheel's come off," he said forlornly.

"How did that happen?"

"It's my fault. I meant to tighten the bolts but forgot all about it as we were in a rush to get away."

"We were only in a rush because we had to persuade Hector to go – so it's his fault," said Whitby.

"It's my fault because I chose this road," said Christopher Rabbit.

Caravan Bear held up his paw. "All right," he said. "Never mind whose fault it was, what are we going to do? I can't mend it until it gets light and we can't sleep in the caravan now – and, in any case, it ought to be moved off the road in case there's traffic."

"And it's started to snow," said Hector gloomily.

"All right for you with your nice new coat," Whitby retorted.

While this was going on, Christopher Rabbit had been looking up the track.

"There's a light up there," he cried. "I think it's a farmhouse. Perhaps whoever lives in it can help us. I'll go if you like."

"I'll come with you," said Whitby and they set off.

Some while later they came back with the farmer, who examined the wheel, tut-tutted under his breath, and said he'd drag the caravan on to the field with his tractor. "And you can sleep in the barn if you like," he said to the animals. "It's a bit rough but better than sleeping out here."

A short while later, once the caravan had been safely placed in the field, Caravan Bear, Whitby, Christopher Rabbit, and Hector pushed open the doors to the barn and stepped inside.

"Close the door!" said a cow.

"Don't you know it's snowing outside?" said another.

"Of course we do," said Whitby. "That's why we've come in here for some shelter."

"No room," said the first cow.

"No room," repeated the second cow.

"There's plenty of room," said Whitby, looking around the big barn.

"We're very choosy about who we allow to share our barn," said the first cow.

"Very choosy," repeated the second cow.

"Look, we're sorry about this," said Caravan Bear, "but it's only for one night and we won't be any trouble."

"That's what they all say," said the first cow.

"They all say that," said the second cow.

"Would you like me to read you a story?" asked Christopher Rabbit. "It's about a barn, or a stable, which is the same thing."

"No, it's not," said Hector. "A stable is where horses live and is usually a very comfortable place. A barn is a…" He looked around in disgust.

"… very comfortable place where cows live," finished the first cow.

The second cow nodded.

Christopher Rabbit picked up his Bible and turned the pages.

"This was a very special stable, or barn, as it was where God's own Son was born."

"Was that Jesus?" asked Caravan Bear.

"Or Father Christmas?" asked Whitby.

"If you let me begin at the beginning, I'll tell you," Christopher Rabbit replied.

They all made themselves as comfortable as they could in the big barn while the two cows wandered over and a family of field mice crept closer. Three big, hairy spiders spun down their threads to hang right over the Bible, much to Whitby's discomfort as she didn't like spiders. An owl flew in through the open window and perched on the ledge.

"An angel visited Mary and told her that God had chosen her to be the mother of God's Son."

"What's an angel?" asked Whitby.

"It's a messenger from God."

"You mean like the carrier pigeons who carry messages?"

"Usually getting them mixed up," added Caravan Bear.

"Perhaps, but I don't think God's angels get their messages mixed up," Christopher Rabbit replied.

"How did Mary know that the angel really *had* come from God?" asked Whitby.

"I expect the angel made it quite clear."

"I bet it was a bit of a shock for her," the first cow commented.

"It probably was," said Christopher Rabbit. He went on. "Mary was engaged to be married to a man called Joseph,

22

who was a carpenter. An angel visited Joseph and told him that Mary would be having this special baby."

"I bet it was a bit of a shock for Joseph, too," added Caravan Bear.

"Why?"

"Well, there he was – all set to marry Mary, have a big wedding and then have children, and suddenly he finds out that she's about to have a baby who isn't his."

"A bit like the cuckoo," said the owl wisely.

"What about the cuckoo?" asked Whitby.

"Cuckoos lay their eggs in other birds' nests and then expect the other birds to bring them up."

"God isn't a cuckoo and Mary wasn't about to lay an egg," said Christopher Rabbit firmly.

"So how did they end up in a barn?" asked the cow.

"In a barn," echoed the second cow.

"Oh, do shut up," said the first cow.

"Sorry," said the second cow.

"Or a stable," added Hector.

Christopher Rabbit went on. "The Roman emperor told everyone in the country that he was going to hold a census."

"What's that?" asked one of the mice.

"It's the counting of heads," said a sheep who had wandered into the barn along with two others. "Brr, it's freezing out there. Mind if we join you?"

"No," said the first cow.

"Yes," said the second cow, and the sheep joined the group around Christopher Rabbit.

"Everyone was told to go back to where they came from so that they could be counted."

"Why did he need to know how many people there were?" asked one of the sheep.

"He needed to know because then he would know how many people owed him money, which they would have to pay as tax," said Christopher Rabbit. "Mary and Joseph were living in a town called Nazareth and had to go back to a village called Bethlehem. So they set off on the journey. It was a very long way."

"Did they travel in a caravan like ours?" asked Hector.

"Possibly," replied Christopher Rabbit cautiously. "It doesn't say. Mary might have ridden on a donkey."

"Or a horse," said Hector. "Much more reliable means of transport."

"They probably couldn't afford a horse. Donkeys

would have been cheaper."

"Perhaps they hired the donkey," said Caravan Bear.

"Perhaps. Anyway, they arrived in Bethlehem to find the place full of people who'd come back for the census. There wasn't anywhere for them to stay. They were told, at the last inn they tried, that there was no room for them inside but they'd be welcome to sleep in the stable…"

"… or barn…"

"… with the animals."

"They couldn't have made the journey in a caravan, then," said Hector triumphantly. "If they had, they'd have been able to sleep in it."

"Provided the wheel hadn't fallen off," Caravan Bear added sadly.

"So, as they didn't have anywhere else to go, they stayed in the stable…"

"… or barn…"

"And Mary had her baby and laid him in the manger."

"A manger is where the farmer puts our food," objected the first cow.

"I suppose the manger was the only really warm

and dry place to put the baby," Christopher Rabbit said thoughtfully.

"Hold on a minute." The owl put up a wing. "Hold on. I think I'm missing something here. You said that this baby, who was not a cuckoo's egg, was God's own Son. Right?"

"Right."

"In that case, this baby – Jesus, wasn't he called?"

"Yes. The angel had told Mary that would be his name."

"Well, this Jesus was a pretty special baby, right?"

"Right."

"Then how come this special baby was born in all the dirt of a barn – or a stable? Pardon if I'm causing offence," he added to the cow.

"No offence," said the cow. "We don't clean the place. The farmer does."

"Not our job," said the second cow.

"Why wasn't he born in a special place, like a palace?" finished the owl.

Everyone looked at Christopher Rabbit.

"I think," he said at last, "and I might be wrong, but I think that God sent his Son to be for everyone. Not just for kings, or emperors, or important people who live in big houses or palaces, but for everyone, however poor, whatever type of place they live in. I think that's why God's Son was born in a stable among the animals."

There was silence for a while.

"Does that mean, then, that God thinks that we matter?" asked the mouse.

"I think everyone matters to God."

"So what happened next?" asked Whitby.

"That night, an angel visited some shepherds who were looking after their flock of sheep in a nearby field."

"Those angels were pretty busy that night," Hector commented.

"When the angel appeared, the shepherds were terrified."

"I'd be pretty scared if an angel suddenly appeared in this barn," said Whitby.

"Me too," said the mouse. Everyone looked around. The barn was dark and full of shadows. Whitby shivered.

"If an angel appeared, it wouldn't be dark in here, it would be shining with light," said Christopher Rabbit firmly, "and I don't think we'd be scared. But the shepherds were. The angel told them not to be frightened and gave them the good news about Jesus' birth. Then the whole sky was full of angels…"

"How many?" asked the owl.

"I don't know. Lots. They were all praising God and saying that he was making earth's peace with heaven. Then they disappeared…"

"For a rest, I suppose," said Whitby, "after all their hard work."

"And the shepherds decided to go and find the baby."

"Did the sheep go with them?" asked one of the sheep. "We are naturally interested."

"I expect so," said Christopher Rabbit. "I don't think the shepherds would have left them behind. After all, their job was to look after the sheep and see they didn't come to any harm."

The sheep looked pleased.

"Must have been a bit crowded in the stable," said Hector. "What with the animals, Mary, Joseph, the baby, and goodness knows how many sheep and their shepherds."

"The shepherds, and sheep, and all the other animals in the stable looked at the baby, who was asleep in the manger…"

"Does it say in the Bible that he was asleep?" asked the owl.

"No," said Christopher Rabbit.

"Well, my experience of human babies, not that I've had much, I must admit, is that they cry a lot – and I doubt that with all the animals traipsing in and out, the baby Jesus would have had any sleep at all."

"I expect you're right," said Christopher Rabbit. "What it does say is that the shepherds told Mary about the angels and then spread the news to everyone they met."

"… who probably all went to the stable, making it even more crowded," said the first cow. "Not much sleep for anyone that night."

"And that's the end of the story," said Christopher

Rabbit. "Well, not the end, just the beginning really."

"Why?"

"Because Jesus was God's Son. God sent him into the world to teach everyone about what God was like and how we can all belong to God's kingdom. Jesus was sent to show how much God loves and cares for us."

The first cow flicked her tail. "Well, that's all very interesting, and thank you for telling us, but now we'd like to get some sleep. We don't usually have this number of visitors and it's all a bit tiring."

"Tiring," echoed the second cow.

The animals settled down. With so many of them in the barn, it soon became warm and everyone grew sleepy. The spiders made their way back up the silken thread to the rafters, the owl hooted "good night" and flew off, the mice tucked themselves into the hay, and the cows and sheep lay down, breathing softly.

"Do you think the caravan will be all right in the field?" Caravan Bear asked Christopher Rabbit quietly.

"Of course it will!" Whitby spoke loudly.

"A little less noise, if you please!" called one of the cows.

"Would you like me to go and stay with it?" offered

Christopher Rabbit.

"No. But thank you," Caravan Bear replied.

Christopher Rabbit closed his Bible and looked thoughtfully around at the sleeping animals. Lastly he looked at the manger, which was full of hay for the cows, and he thought about a special baby who had been born all those years ago.

"Thank you, God, for giving us Jesus," he said quietly. He closed his eyes and was soon fast asleep.

3

The Good Friend

"Oh look!" shrieked Whitby. She barked loudly, then began running back to the caravan.

"What's wrong?" asked Caravan Bear.

"It's a... a snake!"

"It's only a grass snake," said Christopher Rabbit. "And he's probably having a sleep."

The cold, sleety weather had gone. The sun had come out and it was a hot day. The caravan had been parked in a clearing in a wood; Caravan Bear, Whitby, and Christopher Rabbit had decided to go for a walk, leaving Hector to recover from the journey. "I'm tired and I've done enough walking for the time being," he had said firmly before wandering over to the shade of some trees.

The snake opened one eye. "I was having a nice

doze before you started yelling," he hissed angrily.

"I don't like snakes," said Whitby, keeping at a safe distance.

"I don't like you," said the snake, "but I don't go shouting about it."

He slithered off into the bushes and the animals carried on with their walk.

When they returned to the caravan, Hector was feeling much better.

"Tell us another story," he said when he saw Christopher Rabbit.

"After supper," said Christopher Rabbit firmly.

So after supper they all settled down outside the caravan. Whitby looked around anxiously to see if there were any snakes.

"Perhaps we'd be better indoors," he said nervously.

"No, we won't," said Caravan Bear. "Stop worrying."

"Would you like to hear one of the stories Jesus told?" Christopher Rabbit asked.

"I thought he was a baby in a manger," said Whitby.

"When he grew up, he did all sorts of things," said Christopher Rabbit. "He went around the villages and the towns healing people who were sick. Everywhere he went he told people about God. He was also a great storyteller."

"All right," said Whitby. "Tell us one of Jesus' stories."

Christopher Rabbit settled himself comfortably. "The story begins with a man asking Jesus a question. 'What should I do to get into heaven and live for ever?'

"Jesus said to him, 'What do you think?'

"The man replied, 'Love God and love your neighbour as yourself.'

"'That's right!' said Jesus.

"'But who is my neighbour?' asked the man."

"Bert the badger lives next door to me," said Caravan Bear.

"Mine is Min the cat," said Christopher Rabbit. "But I don't think Jesus meant just the one who lives next door to you. I think he meant more than that. So he told this story to explain what a neighbour should be.

"There was a man who came from a town called Jerusalem. One day he went on a journey to another town called Jericho. It was quite a distance and would take him a few days."

"Why was he going to Jericho?" asked Caravan Bear.

"Perhaps he had business there," said Hector.

"He might have been on a walking holiday," said Whitby, who had forgotten about the snake.

"That's if he *was* walking," said Hector. "He might have been making the journey in a caravan."

"Or on a donkey," said Whitby, thinking of Mary and Joseph on their way to Bethlehem.

"He was walking," said Christopher Rabbit. "Suddenly he was set upon by a group of robbers."

"Why didn't he see them coming?" asked Hector.

"Perhaps he was looking at the ground to make sure he didn't trip over any loose stones."

"Or perhaps he was thinking," said Whitby. "I don't look around when I'm thinking."

"As you're always looking around, does that mean you don't think?" Hector teased.

"I imagine the men had been hiding behind some rocks so the man didn't see them. The robbers beat him, tore his clothes, and then ran off taking all his money and his luggage, leaving him lying bleeding in the gutter."

"Poor man," sighed Whitby.

"Got to be careful nowadays," said Hector. "Nasty people around."

"This wasn't nowadays," said Caravan Bear. "It was thousands of years ago."

"Just goes to show that there's always been nasty people," said Hector.

Everyone agreed.

"A few minutes later a priest came along the road. Guess what he did?"

"Went and helped?" asked Whitby.

"Phoned for an ambulance?" asked Hector.

"They didn't have ambulances then," replied Christopher Rabbit.

"Or phones," said Caravan Bear.

"He crossed the road and passed by on the other side, pretending he hadn't seen him."

"That wasn't a nice thing to do," said Whitby.

"Some time later another man came down the

road. This man was known as a Levite, who was someone who helped the priests with their work. He saw the poor man lying in the gutter – and what do you think he did?"

"Don't know," said Hector.

"Probably the same as the priest," said Caravan Bear.

"Is this a guessing game?" asked Whitby.

"He slowed down, walked closer to have a good look, then went off without helping the man."

"Perhaps he thought the man was having a sleep or something," Caravan Bear suggested.

"Perhaps. But if you'd seen someone who was wounded, bleeding, had his clothes torn off him and was generally in a bad way, would you have just left him?"

Caravan Bear shook his head.

"Then a third man came along the road."

"Busy road," said Whitby.

"This man was a Samaritan. The people listening to Jesus didn't like the Samaritans, and the Samaritans didn't like them. In fact, they hated each other."

"Why?"

Christopher Rabbit shrugged. "Maybe because

they were different. Because they came from different kingdoms. Because they had different customs. Because they just didn't like the look of them."

"Like me and snakes," said Whitby.

"And spiders," added Hector. "You don't like spiders either."

"Anyway, they each thought the other nasty, shifty, and not to be trusted."

"I think snakes are like that," said Whitby. "Never trust a snake. Look how that snake behaved in the Garden of Eden!* I can't think why God created them in the first place. The world would have been better off without them."

"I expect that snakes might think the same about dogs," sniffed Caravan Bear.

"Go on with the story," said Hector.

"The man who'd been injured wasn't a Samaritan, so you would have thought that the Samaritan would have just passed by on the other side as the other two people had done – perhaps even laughed at him lying there."

"And kicked him," said Hector.

"Perhaps. But he didn't. He lifted him up gently, cleaned his face, poured oil and wine on to his

wounds to stop them getting worse, bandaged him, put him on his donkey, and took him to an inn.

"He paid the innkeeper for a room and told him to care for the man until he was better. He said that if he didn't have enough money left for all this, he would pay any more costs the next time he came back that way."

"That was really nice of him," said Hector.

"It was, wasn't it?"

"Especially as the Samaritans weren't expected to do something like that."

"It made it especially nice," said Christopher Rabbit. "After Jesus finished telling that story, he asked those listening to him, 'Which of the three men do you think was a real friend and neighbour to the man who'd been beaten?' "

"Obvious, wasn't it?" said Hector.

"Yes. The man who'd asked the question said, 'The one who helped him.' Jesus told him to go and do the same."

"If a snake were run over by a car and badly injured, would you help him?" Caravan Bear asked Whitby.

"I don't know," said Whitby. "Perhaps, after that story, I'd try."

"Glad to hear it," said a hissing voice. It was the snake. Whitby jumped and ran up to the top step of the caravan.

"I liked that story," said the snake. "You didn't mind me listening in, did you?"

"Of course not," smiled Christopher Rabbit.

"Do you think God wants us to be good to everyone, even the animals we don't like?" asked Hector.

"I think that's what Jesus was saying," said Christopher Rabbit.

"But just suppose," said Whitby, who'd recovered from his fright and had been thinking furiously, "just suppose that when the man got better and carried on with his trip to Jericho, he came across one of the robbers who'd attacked him, and this robber had been run over by…"

"… a donkey," suggested Hector.

"All right, a donkey. The other robbers had run off and left him alone in a pretty bad way with broken bones. Then, let's say, he was found by the man he had attacked. What do you think Jesus would have said the man should have done?"

"Pass," said the snake.

"Do you mean 'pass' as in 'passed by on the

other side'?" asked Hector.

"I mean I don't know," said the snake. "I haven't got a very big brain."

"I think he would have said that the man should have stopped to help the robber," said Caravan Bear.

"So do I," agreed Christopher Rabbit.

"Mmm," pondered Whitby. "Difficult, though. I mean the robber had nearly killed the man and taken all his money and his luggage."

"Isn't being a good neighbour about being kind and caring for everyone?" asked Caravan Bear. "No matter whether you like them or not, or whether they've done bad things to you?"

"I think so," said Christopher Rabbit. "I think Jesus was saying that God cares for everyone and we should try and do that too." He closed the Bible. "Anyone fancy a walk?"

"So long as we don't find any more snakes I've got to be nice to," said Whitby.

The snake laughed and slithered away.

"Thank you, God, for the story Jesus told," Christopher Rabbit said. "It's good to know that you care for all of us."

"Even snakes," added Whitby.

The Sheep Who Went Missing

Whitby sat on the steps of the caravan and watched the sheepdog who was in the next field rounding up a flock of sheep. The dog ran this way and that, sometimes crouching low, sometimes barking, always listening to the farmer's whistles, always on the alert for the odd sheep who wanted to break away from the rest.

"I could do that," Whitby declared.

"Do what?" asked Christopher Rabbit, who was sitting on the step beside her.

"Round up sheep. Look, it's easy."

Christopher Rabbit watched the sheepdog neatly move the flock, running behind the stragglers until all the sheep were inside the sheepfold.

"I don't think it can be *that* easy," he said.

"I'm going to speak to the sheepdog," said Whitby,

jumping down from the steps and running across the field.

The caravan had been parked in the farmer's field for a few days. Every day Caravan Bear, Christopher Rabbit, and Hector had gone off exploring the area, but Whitby had always stayed behind watching the sheepdog. Now she raced across the field, her tail waving wildly.

"Excuse me!" she shouted as she ran. "Excuse me!"

The sheepdog turned. "Hello. Aren't you the dog who's staying in the caravan?"

"Yes," replied Whitby, suddenly feeling a bit shy as she peered up at the large black and white dog. "My name's Whitby."

"You've been watching me work," the dog continued.

"Well, yes – I wondered if you could teach me to be a sheepdog."

The dog laughed. "You've got to be born to it," he said kindly. "I'm not sure it's something you can learn in a few days. Apart from anything else, you have to get the sheep to trust you."

"Can I go and talk to them?" Whitby asked.

"Of course. But don't upset them."

"I won't do that."

The sheepdog smiled and went off toward the farmhouse, while Whitby made her way over to the flock of sheep

"Hello, I'm Whitby."

"Oh yes?" said one of the sheep.

"I'd like to be a sheepdog."

"You like to be a what?"

"A sheepdog."

"Oh you would, would you?"

"Yes."

The sheep began to laugh. "Hear that, you lot? This little dog wants to be a sheepdog!"

The other sheep began to laugh.

"Never heard anything so ridiculous," said one of them, turning her back on Whitby. The rest followed.

"I don't know what I said to upset them," Whitby explained later when she was telling Christopher Rabbit, Caravan Bear, and Hector about it. "I only said I'd like to be a sheepdog. It looks such fun."

"It looks like hard work," said Caravan Bear.

"Skilful work, too," Hector added.

When the others went for a walk, Whitby stayed behind to practise the things she had seen the sheepdog do when rounding up the sheep. After a few tries, she thought she could do it.

By now the flock had been moved into a different field. This was her chance. Excitedly she raced toward the sheep, barking loudly.

The sheep who had spoken to Whitby earlier turned around.

"Just look who's here." She put her head down and began grazing. But the other sheep began to panic.

"Hold on, everyone – it's only a silly little dog!"

The flock didn't listen. Baaing loudly, they scattered across the field. Whitby tried to run around them but it was no use. The more she tried, the more the sheep ran from side to side. Two of them broke through the hedges to run into different fields and one made for a copse of trees.

"Hold on – please stop!" poor Whitby cried. "I only want to help!"

By this time, the farmer and the sheepdog had heard the noise and come running.

"That was a very silly thing to do," said the sheepdog as he neatly rounded up the sheep and quietened them down.

A very sad Whitby was taken back to the caravan, the farmer on one side of her, the sheepdog on the other.

"If there's any more trouble with this dog of yours then you'll be off this farm," the farmer said to Caravan Bear. "You need to keep her under control."

"I'm sorry," Whitby muttered.

Later that night, the animals saw lights moving around the sheep field.

"I wonder what's going on?" said Caravan Bear.

"I think they're searching for a sheep," said Hector, who had good eyesight.

There was a knock on the door.

"We've lost one of our sheep – have you seen her?" asked the farmer.

Whitby went to the door. "I didn't see much as they were all rushing around the field."

"Can't see much in this dark, mind. Have to leave it til morning," the farmer replied.

That night Whitby couldn't sleep. She kept thinking about the sheep who was missing. It was all her fault. At the first sign of light, she crept out of the caravan and went to the sheep field. The sheep were huddled together under a tree and Whitby approached them slowly.

"Oh no – trouble!" said one of the sheep.

"I'm really sorry I frightened you," said Whitby, keeping her distance in order not to scare them again. "I'd like to help find the sheep who's missing."

"She went somewhere over there," said another sheep, nodding toward the copse of trees and bushes.

"Thank you!"

Whitby ran over to the copse and plunged in. It was very dark inside and she soon found herself

tangled in some brambles. Tearing herself free, she plunged on.

A faint cry on her left made her turn.

"Sheep, sheep, are you there?" Whitby called. She ran toward the sound of crying and soon found the sheep in the middle of a thicket of brambles. The more the sheep tried to free herself, the more entangled she became, the sharp thorns tearing at her woolly coat.

"Help! Help!" cried the sheep.

"Just stay there and don't move!" Whitby called before running as fast as she could toward the farm, barking loudly to alert the farmer and sheepdog.

"What's happened?" asked the sheepdog as he and

the farmer came running. Whitby took them to the copse of trees, explaining as they went.

It took the farmer a long time to free the sheep. She was trembling with fright when they got to her and kept twisting and turning in the brambles. The farmer had to cut her woolly coat to free her.

"I suppose I should be grateful," said the farmer, once the sheep was safely back with her flock, "although it was your fault to begin with. Thinking you could be a sheepdog indeed! Perhaps that'll teach you a lesson."

With that, he strode off, his dog at his heels. The sheepdog turned.

"Don't worry," he said to Whitby. "He always gets upset when one of his sheep goes missing."

But Whitby still felt guilty and stayed close to the caravan for the rest of the day.

"I don't think I want to be a sheepdog any more," she said to the others at supper.

"The sheep will be pleased to hear that," said Hector, his nose in a bag of oats.

"I'm sure I could be if only I'd been trained," said Whitby. "Perhaps I'll ask the sheepdog for some lessons."

"I wouldn't do that," Caravan Bear warned.

"We don't want to get thrown off the farm," Hector added.

"You know, what happened makes me think of one of Jesus' stories," said Christopher Rabbit. He opened the Bible. "It's in here somewhere."

"Read it to us," said Caravan Bear.

"It'll stop Whitby pestering the sheepdog," said Hector.

"I wasn't going to pester him," said Whitby angrily. "Just ask politely."

In order to stop any more arguing, Christopher Rabbit began. "Jesus told this story to teach a lesson. He told it to a group of men called Pharisees who thought that because they followed all the religious rules and regulations, they were God's favourites.

"God, they felt, didn't favour anyone who didn't do as they did. So they looked down on these people and called them sinners."

"Does God have favourites?" Whitby asked.

"I don't think God has favourites," said Caravan Bear. "I think he cares for everyone."

"So do I," said Christopher Rabbit. "Anyway, the Pharisees had been whispering about Jesus, saying that he shouldn't eat and talk with sinners. Actually, Jesus seemed to be much more interested in these people, the ones the Pharisees thought were too bad for God to care about.

"So Jesus told them this story: 'If a shepherd has a hundred sheep and one goes missing, shouldn't he leave the ninety-nine and go to look for the one who's gone astray?'"

"I don't see why," said Hector. "If he's already got a big flock, what does it matter if he loses one or two?"

"It mattered to the farmer," said Whitby. "He was out late last night looking for that sheep."

"Jesus went on to say that when the shepherd finds the lost sheep and has carried it home with him, he calls his friends and has a party to celebrate."

"I don't think the farmer will hold a party for the sheep I found," sighed Whitby.

"Or if he does, you won't be invited," said Hector.

"So what was the lesson Jesus was trying to teach?" asked Caravan Bear.

"I think that just as the farmer was really happy over finding the one lost sheep, God is very happy over just one bad person who is really sorry. In fact, he's happier about that one person, more than the ninety-nine who are not bad people."

"I'm really sorry for what I did," said Whitby in a small voice. "And I'd like a party," she added hopefully.

The others laughed.

"There's another story Jesus told, about a woman who lost a coin. She had ten coins but one got lost," said Christopher Rabbit.

"That meant she had nine coins left," said Whitby.

"Was that all the money she had?" asked Hector.

"It might have been."

"She might have been saving for something special," Caravan Bear suggested.

"She might. Anyway, she searched and searched her house looking for it. Even when it grew dark she lit a lamp and tried to spot a gleam of the lost coin."

"Did she find it?" asked Caravan Bear anxiously. "I lost a cup the other day and I couldn't find it anywhere, even though I searched and searched the caravan."

Hector looked uncomfortable. "That might have been the one I knocked off the caravan step," he admitted. "It broke."

"Why didn't you tell me?" asked Caravan Bear angrily.

"I didn't think it mattered," Hector replied.

"It mattered to Caravan Bear," said Whitby.

"When the woman found the lost coin, she was so happy that she called her friends and neighbours to tell them about it and asked them to celebrate with her," Christopher Rabbit went on firmly.

"Perhaps they held a party," Whitby said.

"It's saying the same thing as the sheep story, isn't it?" asked Hector, who was hoping that Caravan Bear would forget about the broken cup. "That God is really happy when even just one person is sorry when they've done bad things. It's as though they've been lost to him, but now he's found them again."

"Yes, I think so," said Christopher Rabbit. He closed the book and stretched. "Anyone want a walk before bed?" he asked.

"As long as we keep away from the sheep," said Hector.

"And cups," said Whitby.

As they walked across the field, Caravan Bear said, "I'm glad God cares for all of us."

And Christopher Rabbit, Hector, and Whitby agreed.

5

The Boastful Pharisee

"Isn't that someone waving at us?" asked Caravan Bear, peering at the road ahead of them.

Christopher Rabbit shaded his eyes against the sun. "I think it is," he said. "Hector, you've got good eyesight – who's that waving at us?"

"I don't know," said Hector, not slackening his pace as he towed the caravan along the road.

"Animals often wave because the caravan looks so nice," said Whitby. "And we look nice as well."

Hector put on a spurt of speed and Caravan Bear, Christopher Rabbit, and Whitby had to hold on tight.

The figure waved even harder.

"It's never…" said Caravan Bear.

"It is," said Whitby gloomily.

"It's Runt!" said Christopher Rabbit. "Hasn't he grown!"

"Isn't he fat!" Whitby corrected.

"Slow down, Hector," Caravan Bear called out. "You don't want to run him over!"

Hector slowed down and stopped. A large pig came puffing up to them, a beaming smile on his face.

"Hello, everyone. How nice to see you."

"Hello, Runt," Caravan Bear replied. "How are you?"

"I'm very well," said Runt. "Very well indeed."

Caravan Bear, Whitby, Christopher Rabbit, and Hector had met Runt on their last trip away in the caravan.* Runt had only been a small pig then, with many older brothers and sisters. Now he was fully grown.

"I hoped I'd see you. Why don't you pitch your caravan in that field over there and we can have a nice talk after supper?"

"I've got to ask the farmer," Caravan Bear replied. "He might not want us."

"Oh, he'll want you," said Runt. "He always does what I say."

"Does he?" Whitby was not impressed. "Why's that?"

"Because he knows that I'm the smartest one around here," Runt replied.

The farmer was happy for them to spend a few nights in his field, and when they had pitched the caravan and had supper, Runt appeared on the steps.

"How are your brothers and sisters?" Caravan Bear asked politely.

"Them? Oh, they've all gone," Runt said. "They were fat and lazy and the farmer decided it wasn't worth feeding them any more."

Whitby looked at the large round figure of Runt, who was blocking the doorway.

"Won't the farmer think the same of you?" she asked.

"Of course not!" Runt seemed surprised at the suggestion. "The farmer won't get rid of me! I'm much too smart. We've got more pigs now. I get to choose them, I'm in charge of them, the farmer relies on me entirely, and the pigs do what I say. Good, isn't it?"

"It might be good for you, but is it good for everyone else?"

Runt looked amazed. "Why should I care about anyone else?" he asked. He looked around at the others. "Look, I'm not a bad pig. I'm just smarter than the rest. I keep one step ahead. Eat or be eaten, that's my motto. Nothing wrong in that, is there?"

No one said anything, because no one could think of anything to say.

"It reminds me of a story in the Bible," Christopher Rabbit said at last. "A story Jesus told about one of those Pharisees from our last story and a tax collector."

"What's a Pharisee?" asked Runt.

"A Pharisee was one of the important religious people in Jesus' time," Christopher Rabbit replied. "This particular one, the one in Jesus' story, went to pray in the Temple. He said, 'Thank you, God, for making me better than other people. Thank you for making me a good man, as well as an important one, who does everything you want him too. I keep all the rules and I give away a tenth of my money to the poor. I'm very much better than criminals and even better than thieves and robbers.'

"When he had finished his prayer, he looked around and found that the only other man who was praying was a tax collector, so he went on to say, 'And thank you that I'm much better than that tax collector

over there. Everyone knows that tax collectors are greedy and dishonest.'"

"Well, I'm glad I'm me and not any other pig," Runt interrupted. "Nothing wrong in that, is there?"

"No, of course not," said Christopher Rabbit. "I'm not comparing you with the Pharisee. I'm just telling a story." He went on reading. "Now the tax collector, who was praying in the Temple, was saying something very different. He beat his chest sorrowfully. And he said, 'I've done lots of bad things, God. Please forgive me.'"

"What sort of bad things did he do?" asked Hector.

"I don't know."

"I don't do bad things," said Runt.

"I've done bad things from time to time," said Christopher Rabbit slowly. "And if I haven't done bad things, I've said them or thought them. I think we all do."

"Except me," said Runt.

"So do we all need to ask God to forgive us?" asked Caravan Bear.

"I think so," said Christopher Rabbit.

"And if we ask him, will he forgive us?"

"If we're really and truly sorry when we do wrong."

"There's no point my asking God to forgive me because I've never, ever done anything wrong," Runt said.

"Haven't you ever been nasty to your brothers and sisters?" Whitby asked.

"Oh, that…" A deep pink blush spread over Runt's face. "Well, that's not being nasty. That's just telling the truth."

"So it's not just what you're like on the outside that matters. It's what you're like on the inside that matters as well. Is that it?" asked Hector.

"I *know* I'm better than everyone else on this farm," insisted Runt positively. "Inside and out."

"You might be better, but isn't Jesus saying that it's better not to be boastful and think we're better, because deep down we've all got faults?" asked Caravan Bear.

"I think so," said Christopher Rabbit. "Jesus asked his listeners, 'Which man's prayers did God answer?'"

"That's easy," said Hector. "The tax collector. The Pharisee wasn't really asking God for anything, was he? He was just saying how good and important he was."

"I've got to go," said Runt, getting to his feet. "I've important work to do."

With that, he went down the steps and across the fields. The others watched him.

"I like Runt – despite everything," said Caravan Bear.

"I don't," said Whitby. "He's stuck-up and boastful and thinks he's the cat's pyjamas!"

Christopher Rabbit laughed. "I don't think cats wear pyjamas," he said.

"You know what I mean!"

"I feel a bit sorry for him," said Hector unexpectedly.

"Why?"

"Well, I think that underneath it all, he's really a bit lonely."

"With all those other pigs?" Whitby said.

"Yes, but as he thinks he's better than them, he can't really be friends with them, can he?"

"I suppose not."

"I don't think he's got any real friends," Caravan Bear said thoughtfully. "Otherwise he wouldn't come and boast to us."

"Perhaps we should try to be his friends," Christopher Rabbit suggested.

"Huh?" said Whitby.

"Perhaps we should ask God to help him be a kinder, nicer pig," said Caravan Bear.

"Perhaps," said Whitby uncertainly.

"I think we should," said Christopher Rabbit firmly. "Dear God, we know that you love Runt, but we find him really difficult. And maybe he is a bit lonely. Please help him learn how to be kind and think about other people so that he can make real friends."

"And now perhaps it's time we went to sleep," said Caravan Bear.

Which is what they did.

6

The Unmerciful Servant

Christopher Rabbit, Caravan Bear, and Whitby were just finishing their breakfast when they heard someone coming up the steps to the caravan. It opened before any of them had time to reach the door. Runt stood in the entrance.

"It's polite to knock first," said Whitby, with her mouth full.

"Is it?" Runt looked around at them, surprised. "No one knocks at the door of my pigsty."

"Would you like a drink?" asked Caravan Bear.

"No. I'd like another story," replied Runt.

Christopher Rabbit was surprised. "Would you? I thought you didn't like the stories."

"I might not agree with them but I like to hear you tell them," Runt said. "It reminds me of my mother telling me stories when I was a piglet."

"We're going down to the river," said Whitby. "Caravan Bear is going to teach me how to fish."

"Caravan Bear's not very good at fishing," said Hector, poking his nose in through the window. "Last time he tried, he didn't catch anything."

"Are *you* any better?" asked Caravan Bear. "And I only didn't catch any fish because I was listening to Christopher Rabbit's story."

"I'll come down to the river with you and you can tell another story," Runt said to Christopher Rabbit.

"It's polite to ask Christopher Rabbit if he minds telling us a story," barked Whitby.

Christopher Rabbit laughed. "I don't mind at all."

So they cleared up the breakfast dishes and made some lunch, because as Caravan Bear said, "As soon as we get there, we'll be hungry and want something to eat." Then they set off across the fields and down to the river, armed with fishing rods and a big hamper of food.

Once they found a good spot, they sat down. Caravan Bear and Whitby cast their fishing lines into the water and Christopher Rabbit took out the Bible and began to read.

"This story is about an unmerciful servant," he began.

"What does unmerciful mean?" Whitby asked, turning around.

"It means not having mercy on others – not being kind, not showing them love and understanding."

"Can you show a bit of understanding, Whitby, and stop waving your rod around?" cried Caravan Bear "You nearly poked my eye out!"

"Sorry."

Christopher Rabbit went on. "Peter, a friend of Jesus, asked how many times he had to forgive someone who had done something bad to him. 'Should it be even as many as seven times?' he asked.

"Jesus told him that seven times wasn't enough. He said that Peter should forgive as many as seventy-seven times."

Runt was shaking his head.

"I don't forgive," he said bluntly. "When someone's nasty to me I don't forgive them at all, let alone forgive them seventy-seven times."

"Why not?" asked Christopher Rabbit.

"Because they'd think I was weak," Runt said. "And because they wouldn't deserve it."

"Why seventy-seven times?" asked Whitby. "What about the seventy-eighth time?"

"I think it means more times than you can count – which means always," Caravan Bear said thoughtfully.

"I agree. You should always forgive." Hector put his head down and began munching at the long grass. "It's hard, though."

"You haven't got anything to forgive," Whitby teased. "We treat you really well. We're kind to you and understand when you take off down the road at top speed and shake us all to bits!"

"My old master used to beat me," said Hector, "and I'm not sure I can forgive him."

Everyone was silent for a moment, then Christopher Rabbit continued.

"Jesus told a story to explain what he meant about forgiveness. He said that the kingdom of heaven is like a king who wanted his servants to pay him back the money they'd borrowed from him."

"Why did the king lend them money in the first place?" asked Hector. He leaned over Christopher Rabbit's shoulder, his nose almost inside the book.

"I don't know," Christopher Rabbit replied. "Perhaps they wanted to buy something big, like a house, and hadn't saved up enough. And if you wouldn't mind moving your head a little, Hector, I'll read on."

"Perhaps Hector is trying to read," said Caravan Bear.

"Go on with the story," Runt demanded.

"One of the servants owed the king ten thousand bags of gold. A huge amount."

"Bit stupid to lend his servant all that money,"

said Runt. "You wouldn't catch me doing it if I were king."

"Well, the servant couldn't pay back anything like that amount, so the king ordered that he and his wife and his children should all be sold as slaves in order to repay the debt."

"Bit tough," said Whitby.

"Just fair," said Runt.

"The servant fell on his knees. 'Please be patient with me,' he pleaded, 'and I will pay back everything!'

The king looked at him and felt sorry for him, so he told him that he wouldn't have to pay back anything at all – and he let him go."

"That was nice of him," said Hector.

"It was stupid of him," said Runt. "I mean, if the king was owed the money, he should have been paid back."

"I think that the king showed that he was a good and kind man," said Caravan Bear. "He had mercy on his servant."

"What happened next?" asked Hector.

"Well, the servant went off, very relieved. As he

went, he met another servant and remembered that *this* man owed *him* a hundred silver coins. He grabbed the servant by the scruff of his neck, nearly choking him.

"'Pay me what you owe me!' he shouted. The man fell on his knees and begged him, 'Be patient and I'll pay it all back!'"

"That was what the first servant had said to the king," Whitby said.

"That's right."

"So did the first servant do as the king had done?"

"What was that?" asked Hector, swishing a fly away with his tail.

"You're not LISTENING, Hector!" Whitby shouted.

"And you're not fishing, Whitby," said Caravan Bear. "And if you shout like that, you'll scare all the fish away."

"The king told the servant that he forgave him for not having the money to repay his debt – and then let him go completely free," said Whitby slowly. "*Now* do you understand?"

"Of course I understand all that," said Hector. "I might be a bit slow, but I'm not stupid. I just got confused with all these servants and I was distracted by the fly." He swished his tail again.

"I'll explain," said Runt importantly. "Servant number one owed the king a fortune and couldn't pay it back. The king forgave him and said that he wouldn't have to repay it.

"Then servant number one met servant number two. Servant number two owed servant number one  some money and couldn't pay it back." He turned to Christopher Rabbit. "Did servant number one do the same as the king and forgive servant number two?"

"No," replied Christopher Rabbit. "He refused. He had the man thrown into prison until he could pay his debt."

"What an awful thing to do," said Whitby, who, by this time had forgotten all about fishing.

"Whitby! You've dropped the rod!" shrieked Caravan Bear. He began wading into the river. "That was my special rod, and you promised to take care of it!"

"I'm sorry," said Whitby. She ran into the river and returned, wet and dripping, with the rod in her mouth.

"Oh, all right," Caravan Bear grumbled. "I forgive you." He put down his own rod. "I give up. I can't concentrate anyway."

"Can we have something to eat then?" asked Whitby. "I'm starving."

"Let's hear the end of the story first," said Runt. "It's really interesting."

The others looked at him in surprise.

"When all the other servants heard what had happened, they were very angry with servant number one. They went to the king and told him everything.

"The king was furious. He ordered the first servant to be brought to him. 'You wicked man,' he said. 'I let you off your debt to me because you begged me to and I felt sorry for you. I had mercy on you. Shouldn't you have shown the same mercy to your fellow servant?'

"In his anger, he threw the man into prison to be punished until he paid back all the money he owed. Jesus ended the story by saying, 'This is how God will treat you if you don't forgive others from your heart.'"

Christopher Rabbit closed the Bible.

"If Jesus said that you should keep on forgiving, shouldn't the king have forgiven the wicked servant for a second time?" asked Runt.

Christopher Rabbit thought about it.

"Yes, if the servant had learned his lesson and been sorry about how he'd behaved."

"I think the story is saying that we should treat others as we'd like them to treat us," said Caravan Bear. "The king was merciful and forgiving to the servant who owed him a lot – and you would have expected the servant to be so grateful that he would have treated the other servant in the same way. But he didn't."

"I can't forgive," said Runt.

"Who can't you forgive?" asked Caravan Bear.

"My brothers and sisters."

"Why?"

"They were horrid to me when I was little. They grabbed my food and pushed me in the mud and kept me prisoner in the pigsty. I hated them. I still do."

"Even though they're not here any more?"

Runt didn't answer.

"I don't think it's always easy to forgive,"

Christopher Rabbit said slowly. "But that's what God wants us to do. If you think about it, God forgives us all the time – so shouldn't we try to do the same?"

"But I don't need forgiving," Runt said. "I've already told you. I've never done anything bad."

"Never?" asked Hector.

Runt was silent.

"Let's have some food," said Caravan Bear, opening the hamper. "And then shall we go for a walk?"

"No more fishing?" asked Hector.

"No more fishing," said Caravan Bear firmly. "At least, not while Christopher Rabbit is telling a story."

While Christopher Rabbit and Whitby were getting food out of the hamper, Runt wandered away – and Christopher Rabbit followed him.

"Aren't you staying to have something to eat?" he asked.

"You don't want me," said Runt.

"Oh, yes we do," said Christopher Rabbit. "Of course we do. Please stay."

He looked at the pig. Runt was staring at the ground, a very sad expression on his face.

"I didn't like them because they bullied me, but now they're gone, I don't have anyone else."

"Yes, you have. You have us, when we visit. What about all the other pigs on the farm?"

"They're scared of me."

"Perhaps if you were kind to them, they'd be kind to you."

"Perhaps. I'll try."

With that, he shrugged his massive shoulders and went back to the other pigs. Christopher Rabbit watched him go.

"Please God," he said, "help Runt. Help him be kinder to others and help him forgive his brothers and sisters. He'll be a much happier pig if he does. And please, God, help us all to forgive when others are unkind or hurtful."

He stood for some moments, looking at the river. Then he walked back. He was hungry and ready for some food.

The Poor Rich Man

As soon as the caravan reached the seaside, Caravan Bear, Christopher Rabbit, and Hector set up for a few days' stay.

But the sight of the golden sand and the sea sparkling in the summer sun was too much for Whitby. She left the others and ran off, sniffing the salt-tanged air and enjoying the feel of sand under her paws.

It was still early in the morning and, for a while, Whitby had the beach to herself. But not for long. A man and a woman soon appeared with a dog walking sedately beside them. Whitby stared then raced across the sand.

"Wuff!" she called. "Hello! I'm Whitby and I've just arrived! Who are you and what's your name?"

The dog turned and Whitby stopped. She had never seen such a strange dog before. It had tight, white curls all over its body, although its ears were long and fluffy. The fur on the top of its head was adorned with a pink ribbon. A pink bow was tied around its tail.

Despite it being a warm day, the dog was wearing a thick coat. A pink and green collar around the dog's neck was studded with brightly shining stones that glinted like jewels in the sun.

"Why are you wearing a coat?" Whitby demanded.

"That's a lot of questions," the dog replied. "My name is Ermintrude and I'm a poodle. I'm wearing a coat because I've just had a treatment at the BDS and mustn't get my fur dirty."

"What's the BDS?"

"It's the Beautiful Dog Shop," Ermintrude replied, shaking her head so that her ribbon waved around. "My owners think me a beautiful dog."

"What's a treatment?" Whitby replied, unimpressed.

"BDS trims my fur, and gives me a lovely bubble bath and a massage. My fur is blow-dried and my topknot styled. Once a month my nails are clipped."

"How often do you go?"

"Once a week."

Whitby was amazed.

"I know what you're thinking," said Ermintrude. "It *is* expensive, but then I'm a very famous poodle. My owners put me in for all the dog shows and I always win. My picture has been in all the papers. Haven't you seen it?"

Whitby shook her head. "Do you *always* win?"

"Yes."

"What would happen if you lost?"

Ermintrude considered this. "I don't know," she said at last. "I don't like to think about it."

Suddenly she looked scared. "I expect my owners would sell me," she whispered.

"Ermintrude!"

The man and woman had stopped and were looking back.

"Come along, Ermin! Leave that nasty little dog alone. You don't know where it's been! You don't want to pick up any fleas!"

Ermintrude obediently began to walk away.

"Can I see you again?" Whitby called.

"Why don't you come to my house?" Ermintrude called back. "It's third on the left along the seafront. Come after lunch when my owners have a sleep and I'll show you my room and all my toys. It'll be fun. I've never shown them to anyone before." She glanced around at her owners. "But you'll have to be quiet."

"Can I bring my friends?" asked Whitby.

"Any friends of yours will be welcome," said Ermintrude.

Whitby couldn't get back to the caravan fast enough to tell the others about this strange dog.

"I don't think Hector should go," said Caravan Bear.

"Why not?" asked Hector.

"Because you're too big to go inside anyone's house," Caravan Bear replied firmly.

Hector went off in a sulk.

After lunch Christopher Rabbit, Caravan Bear, and Whitby walked down the seafront to the third house on the left. Ermintrude was waiting at the door. Her coat had been removed but she still wore ribbons on her head and tail. On her paws were small pink bootees. Her face dropped when she saw Caravan Bear and Christopher Rabbit.

"I thought your friends were dogs," she said.

"Oh, no," said Whitby. "This is Caravan Bear and Christopher Rabbit. We left Hector the horse behind."

Ermintrude looked relieved. "Well, come in, but make sure that you are very quiet."

They trooped in after her.

Ermintrude pushed open a door and Christopher Rabbit, Caravan Bear, and Whitby gasped.

It was a large room. In one corner was a built-in shower and in another was a comfortable bed.

Green, pink, and red coats were stacked on shelves above piles of collars and leads. Dog bowls were placed on a low shelf, full of enticing food. The rest of the room was taken up by toys. There were toys everywhere. The friends didn't know where to look first.

"Are all these yours?" asked Caravan Bear in awe.

"Oh, yes. My owners always buy me the latest. I get tired of them very quickly."

"Can we – may we – have a play with some of them?" Whitby asked.

"Why not? As long as you don't make a noise." Ermintrude looked anxiously at the door. "My owners wouldn't like to find you here."

"Why?"

"They don't like me mixing with other dogs – and they'd be very angry if they found I'd been entertaining a bear and a rabbit."

"Doesn't that make it a bit lonely for you?" asked Christopher Rabbit gently.

Ermintrude shrugged. "I suppose it does. But then I'm very grateful to my owners for the lovely life I have." She laughed. "I do like having new things. Don't you?"

"Oh, yes," breathed Whitby, "but I don't often get them."

They spent a wonderful hour, playing with the toys. They threw balls of all shapes and sizes at each other, found fun bones buried under cushions that made a noise when sat on, squeezed the toy duck that quacked, and ate all the food.

They were quite sorry when it was time to go, but Ermintrude had heard sounds in the next room that meant that her owners were waking up.

"I'll be walking on the beach tomorrow," she said as they went. "But be careful not to talk to me when my owners are near."

"Could you come to supper with us in the caravan?" asked Caravan Bear.

Ermintrude's face lit up. "I'd love to." Then her face fell. "But I can't, I'm afraid. My owners would be so worried if I went out by myself. They'd probably call the police. I'm worth a lot of money and someone might want to steal me."

After the friends had returned to the caravan and told Hector about their afternoon, they fell silent.

Whitby sighed.

"I'd love to live like that," she said.

"Would you?" asked Hector. "Sounds more like a prison to me."

"They're always buying things for her. And she's so well looked after. Fancy having a bubble bath and massage every week!"

"I wouldn't like it," said Hector firmly.

"No, but you're not a poodle."

"Neither are you. And you're not that fond of having baths anyway," Hector retorted.

"What's the point in wanting more and more things? I don't think it makes you happy."

"Ermintrude seems happy."

"I hope she is."

They were all silent.

"I'll tell you a story, shall I?" asked Christopher Rabbit.

"Yes, do," said Hector. "I must say I'm sick of hearing all about how wonderful those toys were."

Christopher Rabbit fetched his Bible.

"I'll tell you the story about the rich fool," he said. "One day a man said to Jesus, 'My father's just died and my brother won't divide the family property between us. Please tell him it's not fair.'

"Jesus explained that it wasn't his job to settle

family arguments. Then he said to the crowd, 'Be careful not to become greedy. Life is more than the things you own.'

"He went on to tell them a story about a rich farmer who had had a wonderful harvest. It was such a big harvest that he didn't have enough barns in which to store it all."

"Why didn't he build some more?" asked Caravan Bear.

"That's exactly what he planned to do," said Christopher Rabbit. "He walked around his farm, looking at his barns, and shook his head. The barns just weren't big enough to take all the grain from the splendid harvest. So he decided to pull them all down and rebuild them. Perhaps, he thought, he might build one or two more."

"Why pull down the barns that were already there?" Caravan Bear asked.

"Perhaps they were old and rotten?" Hector suggested.

"Perhaps," Christopher Rabbit agreed. "They might have been there for years and years. The farmer made his plans, rubbing his hands. He would build really big barns, barns large enough to take all the

grain from his amazing harvest. Then, he thought, he would have enough to live on for years. He could retire, take it easy, enjoy himself."

"Go on holiday, like us," said Caravan Bear.

"Nothing wrong with planning ahead," said Hector. "Wasn't he just being like Joseph in that story you told us last year?* You know, when he advised the king of Egypt to store the grain from the good years of harvest so they would have plenty when there was a famine?"

Whitby turned to look at Hector.

"Sometimes you amaze me, Hector," she said. "Fancy you remembering the stories Christopher Rabbit told us last year!"

"Why not? I might be a bit slow but once I'm told things, I remember them," Hector said placidly.

"I think there's a difference," said Christopher Rabbit slowly. "Joseph was thinking about storing enough grain to feed all the people in Egypt when there was a famine. The farmer in Jesus' story was just thinking of himself."

"You mean he was just being greedy?" asked Caravan Bear.

"And selfish. Anyway, that very night God spoke

to the farmer," Christopher Rabbit went on. "He told the man that he was being a fool, for that very night he was going to die."

"Yes, but the farmer didn't know that when he made his plans," said Hector stubbornly. "So I don't think he was a fool at all."

"What would happen to all the grain?" asked Caravan Bear.

"Perhaps his sons and daughters would have it," said Whitby.

"I hope they wouldn't squabble about it, like the person who spoke to Jesus about the family property," said Caravan Bear.

"Jesus said that everyone who spends their life wanting to be rich, wanting more and more, is missing the point. They aren't being rich in the things that really matter."

"What really matters, then?" asked Whitby.

"Trusting in God."

"What does that mean?"

"Well, we can't take any of our possessions with us when we die, so perhaps we shouldn't worry about them too much – or worry about getting more and more of them," said Christopher Rabbit.

"I don't have any possessions to worry about," said Whitby. "But that doesn't mean I wouldn't like them. Or at least some of them. Like that wonderful ball we saw at Ermintrude's house, the one on the end of a string that bounced back at you."

"I wouldn't like to be Ermintrude," said Caravan Bear thoughtfully. "I know she's got everything she wants, but she doesn't have any friends, has she? And you told us that she was worried about what would happen when she was too old to win prizes at dog shows."

"Jesus went on to say to his friends that they would be happiest if they learned to trust in God for the things they need day by day. He told them not to worry about things like where their next meal would come from or whether they would be able to afford new clothes."

"I'm glad I don't wear clothes," said Hector. "I don't have to worry about them."

"Yes, you do!" said Caravan Bear. "What about that lovely coat Whitby and I gave you for Christmas?"

"Oh. I forgot about that."

"You just said you were good at remembering," teased Whitby.

"Did I? I forget." Hector smiled and the other animals laughed.

"Shall I go on?" Christopher Rabbit asked. "Jesus said that God takes care of the birds who don't earn any money. He said that God clothes the flowers in beautiful clothes for nothing, so God will see that you have the things you need. He told the crowds that they should always put God first and God will take care of them."

The following morning the friends were on the beach, Whitby running ahead chasing a butterfly. When she saw Ermintrude and her owners, she ran up, barking happily.

"Hello, Ermintrude! What a lovely morning!"

"Oh dear, it's that nasty little dog again!" said the woman. "Come, Ermin!"

She turned away. Ermintrude shook her head at Whitby and walked off behind her owner without saying a word.

"Why wouldn't she speak to us?" Whitby demanded when Christopher Rabbit, Caravan Bear, and Hector had joined her.

"She was probably told not to," said Caravan Bear.

"Yes," said Whitby. "Well, I'm glad I'm not her. I

can do without the toys and the Beautiful Dog Shop and winning prizes. It's more fun having friends to play with! Race you to the sea!" she shouted and ran off. Hector galloped after her.

"Poor Ermintrude," said Caravan Bear.

"Yes," agreed Christopher Rabbit. "Poor Ermintrude. Please look after her, God, and thank you for Jesus' story that shows us what makes us really happy."

Then Christopher Rabbit and Caravan Bear ran off toward the sparkling sea where Whitby was running along the water's edge, Hector galloping beside her.

The Wise and Foolish Builders

It was late in the evening and Caravan Bear, Christopher Rabbit and Whitby were very tired of travelling. At last Hector turned off the road, towed the caravan over a bridge and up a hill, and stopped.

"That's it," he said. "I'm not towing this caravan any further. I'm tired and I'm hungry."

"We're all tired and hungry," said Whitby.

"Maybe, but you haven't been pulling this caravan for miles," Hector retorted.

Caravan Bear quickly released the horse from between the shafts of the caravan and gave him a large bucket of oats.

"Where are we?" asked Christopher Rabbit, looking around.

"I don't know, because we took a wrong turn a few

miles back," said Caravan Bear.

"No, we didn't," Hector mumbled through a mouthful of oats.

"Yes, we did," said Whitby. "Caravan Bear said 'turn right' and you turned left."

Hector buried his face in the bucket and didn't reply.

"Well, now we're here…" Caravan Bear began.

"Wherever 'here' is," said Whitby.

"… we might as well make the most of it. I'll make supper."

"I'll help," offered Christopher Rabbit.

"No, you tell us a story," said Whitby. "We haven't had a story for a few days."

"Yes," agreed Caravan Bear. "Tell us another of Jesus' stories while I make some food. And Whitby can help me."

"Oh all right," said Whitby, "but make it a short story as I'm starving."

Christopher Rabbit took out his Bible and opened it.

"Here's a short story. Jesus said that everyone who hears what he teaches and puts it into practice is like a wise man who builds his house on a rock. If there's

a storm and it pours with rain and the winds howl around and the river floods, the house will be safe because it's been built on a solid foundation."

"What did Jesus mean?" asked Whitby, her mouth full.

"I think he meant that a wise person who follows the words of Jesus and trusts in God will be like the man who built his house on a rock. Whatever happened to him, he would be safe with God."

Caravan Bear had finished cooking and was dishing up. "Food's ready – that's if Whitby has left us anything to eat!"

"I've only eaten a bit," Whitby protested.

"Jesus went on to say that everyone who hears what he's saying but does not do anything about it is like a man who builds his house upon sand," Christopher Rabbit went on. "When there's a storm and it pours with rain and the winds howl around and the river floods, the house built on sand will fall down."

"Why?" asked Whitby.

"That's pretty obvious," said Hector, who had finished his meal of oats and was listening to the story, his head stuck through the window of the caravan. "Sand is all squishy. If it's dry, it moves when you walk on it – and if it's wet, you can get bogged down in it. I got stuck on some dry sand once and it was very scary. My hooves just seemed to sink in."

"I don't think it's that obvious," said Caravan

Bear. "Lots of people build their homes on weak foundations…"

"… so do animals…" agreed Christopher Rabbit.

"… and birds…" said Whitby. "I know a couple

of starlings who spent a long time building their nest on a very thin branch of a tree because they liked the view, but the branch broke when it was windy and their nest fell to pieces."

"Were they hurt?" asked Hector.

"Not really, but they made a lot of noise."

"Starlings are noisy," Hector added.

"I told them it wasn't a safe branch to build their nest on, but they wouldn't listen."

"That's starlings for you. Too busy making a noise to listen to anyone else."

"It reminds me of Frank," said Christopher Rabbit after a pause.

"Who's he?" asked Whitby.

"He's a mole. It happened last spring when Frank wanted to get away from the other animals."

"Why did he want to do that?"

"I don't really know, but I don't think moles really get on with other moles. Anyway, Frank loves tunnelling so he tunnelled and tunnelled through the earth, then under some clay – which, he said, was hard work and very sticky.

"When he came to the end of the clay, the soil became nice and easy to tunnel through. So Frank tunnelled and tunnelled until he came to a spot that he thought would make a comfortable home. When he'd finished, he moved his family into it."

"And what happened?"

"Unfortunately he'd made his home under some wet sand. When the sand dried out, his home collapsed."

"Was his family all right?"

"Oh, yes. But Frank had to start tunnelling all over again."

"Just like Jesus said in the story," said Whitby.

"I don't think Jesus was talking about Frank the mole," said Hector.

They were all silent for a moment, thinking of animals and birds who had built homes in unsafe places.

Christopher Rabbit said at last, "What I think Jesus was saying was that people who listened to him might have agreed with what he was saying but didn't try to put what he said into practice."

"Like Hector, who heard Caravan Bear say 'turn right' but then turned left," said Whitby.

"I didn't hear Caravan Bear say anything of the sort," snorted Hector.

"That's because you didn't want to hear," said Whitby. "I know why you turned left instead of right. It was because there was a nice-looking field on the left with lovely long grass!"

"To get back to what Christopher Rabbit was saying," said Caravan Bear hurriedly, "do you mean that people – or animals or birds – who built their homes on unsafe ground – or underground in the case of Frank – might listen to Jesus and agree with what he said, and that was fine as long as everything was going well? But when things weren't going well they went to pieces, because they didn't have any proper foundation, any real belief or trust in God, just like houses built on sand?"

"Or in Frank's case, *under* sand," said Whitby.

"I think so," said Christopher Rabbit.

"Well that's a nice, short story," said Hector. "I'm off for a sleep." He wandered away to the other side of the hill.

Just then Christopher Rabbit, Whitby, and Caravan Bear felt the caravan give a sudden lurch.

Christopher Rabbit and Caravan Bear fell off their

seats while Whitby, who was sitting on the hearthrug, slid right across the floor.

Plates, cups, and saucers began to fall off the shelves. The caravan lurched again and the animals clutched hold of each other.

"Is it an earthquake?" squeaked Whitby.

The caravan began to move!

"Help!" shouted Whitby.

"Help!" cried Caravan Bear.

"Help!" called Christopher Rabbit, holding tightly on to his Bible with one hand and clutching the leg of the table with the other.

The caravan gathered speed!

Hector came galloping over. "What's going on?" he shouted.

Caravan Bear struggled to the door of the caravan and managed to push it open.

"The caravan's running away!"

The caravan began to roll down the hill.

"We'll end up in the river!" cried Christopher Rabbit.

Faster and faster it went…!

… and then it started to slow down.

It slowed some more and finally came to a stop

right at the water's edge. Its bright yellow wheels were firmly stuck in the sand.

The three animals came tumbling out as Hector raced up to them.

"What happened?" asked Christopher Rabbit.

Caravan Bear looked back up the hill. "I'm sorry," he said. "It's my fault. We parked on a hill and I forgot to put bricks under the wheels to stop it from running away. I'm so sorry."

Christopher Rabbit walked around the caravan, examining it. "There doesn't seem to be any damage," he said. "And Hector can pull us out of the sand in the morning."

"Thanks," said Hector sarcastically. "I'll look forward to that."

"We'll all help," said Caravan Bear.

Whitby suddenly sat down and began to laugh.

"It's a bit like the story, isn't it?" she said. "Jesus should have added that caravans had to be made secure when parked on hills!"

Christopher Rabbit and Hector started laughing and, after a moment, Caravan Bear joined in. They lay on the sand and laughed and laughed.

"It was a good story," said Hector. "Jesus told lots

of good stories, didn't he?"

"Yes, he did," said Christopher Rabbit. "Thank you, Jesus, for the story about the wise and foolish builders. I don't think we'll forget it in a hurry!"

"I'm sure we won't," said Whitby, and they all began laughing once more.

9

The Lost Son

"Out of the way!" shouted Hector as he clip-clopped smartly along the road, the caravan bouncing up and down behind him.

"Wha... who...?" croaked the pheasant, skittering from side to side in a panic.

"We're coming through!" Hector shouted as he and the caravan bore down on the pheasant at an alarming rate.

Whitby barked, Caravan Bear closed his eyes, and Christopher Rabbit called, "Fly, why don't you fly!"

The pheasant gave one startled glance at the caravan, then, at the very last minute, spread his wings and flew over the hedge that bordered the road.

"Phew – that was close," said Caravan Bear.

They rode on for a few miles then stopped by the

roadside for some lunch.

"Why don't pheasants like to fly?" asked Whitby as she chewed on a bone. She had eaten all the meat off it some time ago, but liked to carry on chewing.

"Brinkmanship," said Hector briefly, closing his eyes.

"What do you mean?"

"It's the only exciting thing that happens to them," said Hector. "Bit of a boring life really, being a pheasant."

"How do you know?"

"Well, stands to reason. All they do is eat, get fat, waddle around, and then get shot. No wonder they play silly and dangerous games with the traffic. Only bit of fun they have."

"Poor things," said Christopher Rabbit.

"Should we have invited the pheasant to come with us," Whitby wondered, "so he could have a few adventures?"

Caravan Bear started to clear away the lunch dishes. "Too late now. And I hope we don't have another adventure like last night. That was a bit too exciting for me!"

They soon packed up. Hector was hitched to

the caravan, Caravan Bear, Christopher Rabbit and Whitby sat on the steps, and Hector set off down the road, slowly for once as he had had a lot to eat for lunch and felt a bit sleepy.

Caravan Bear, Christopher Rabbit, and Whitby also felt sleepy. They were full of food, the sun was shining, and Hector was jogging quietly along. Soon they were fast asleep.

They were woken much later by the roar of traffic.

"Where are we?" mumbled Caravan Bear.

"I don't know," said Hector. "We're in the middle of a town. I did ask where I should go but as none of you answered, I just carried on."

They had stopped at a set of traffic lights showing red. A queue of cars began to build up behind them.

The traffic lights went from red to red-and-amber to green.

"What should I do?" asked Hector, beginning to panic as the queue behind him grew longer. He wasn't used to towns. Drivers began hooting their horns.

Whitby jumped off the steps and ran around the back of the caravan, barking loudly.

"Whitby!" shouted Caravan Bear, "Come back! You'll get run over!"

"Just go!" Christopher Rabbit urged Hector.

The horse set off with a jerk as Whitby, still barking, jumped back onto the caravan steps.

As they drove through the town, the traffic grew heavier. The pavements were crowded with people who spilled over into the roads. Some of them ran in front of the caravan; others stopped, pointed, and took photographs. Shops and houses seemed to tower over them.

"I don't like this," said Whitby.

"Think I do?" Hector replied.

"Can't you just drive out of the town?"

"I would if I knew the way!"

Hector swerved to avoid a cyclist and nearly ran into a car. The driver shouted.

"Look," said Caravan Bear, "there are some trees ahead. And grass. And there's an entrance. Go in there."

Clip clop, clip clop! Hector went faster and faster. Across the road and into the entrance. He was trembling when he came to a stop.

"Don't want to do that again in a hurry!"

Christopher Rabbit looked around. "I think we're in a park. Perhaps we can stay here tonight."

After a rest and something to eat, everyone felt much better.

"How about a story?" asked Whitby.

"All right," said Christopher Rabbit. He pulled his Bible toward him and opened it.

Everyone settled down.

"This story is about a farmer who had two sons. Both of them worked on the farm, caring for the animals, digging, planting, and sowing. One of the sons was happy but the other son wasn't. He went to his father and told him that he wanted to leave home.

"'I want to travel,' he said. 'I want some change and excitement. I want to have some adventures.'"

"Like us," said Whitby.

"He asked his father for some money. 'You know that when you die, I'll get half the farm for myself? Well, I'd like to have that money now.'"

"Was his father upset that he wanted to leave?" asked Hector.

"I expect he was but he understood how his son

felt, so he gave him money. A few days later the son was on his way."

"Didn't the other brother want to leave the farm as well?" asked Whitby.

"No. He was happy where he was."

"The first son's journey took him a long way from home, into another country. He saw new sights, did a lot of new things, and had many adventures. He made new friends. Some of the things he did were bad and some of his new friends were bad too. Maybe they just made friends with him because he had lots of money. But he soon spent the money his father had given him."

"What did he spend it on?" asked Caravan Bear.

"On anything and everything. He probably spent money on his new friends, treating them to expensive meals and presents."

"I wish I had friends who gave me nice meals

and presents," Whitby said wistfully.

"What do you mean?" asked Caravan Bear. "You get lots of good food!"

"What sort of presents do you want?" asked Hector.

Whitby thought for a moment. "I don't know. Perhaps a squeaky duck like Ermintrude's. Or a smart collar. Or…"

"Wait til your birthday," said Caravan Bear firmly. "And I don't suppose they were real friends, either. You said some of them were bad. Real friends don't want expensive meals or presents."

"I suppose not," Whitby said, not completely convinced.

Christopher Rabbit went on. "What do you think happened next?"

"No idea," said Whitby, who was still thinking about squeaky ducks and smart collars.

"One of his new friends stole his money?" Hector suggested.

"No."

"Did he run out of money?" asked Caravan Bear.

"Yes. He spent all his money and had nothing left."

"What about his friends? Didn't they help?"

"I don't expect so, because as soon as he ran out of money, there was a terrible famine in the country."

"What's a famine?" asked Hector, who was enjoying munching some oats.

"It means no oats," said Caravan Bear.

"It means not much food of any sort," said Christopher Rabbit. "I imagine his new friends were more worried about how they would get enough food for themselves and their families. They wouldn't have had time for anything else."

"And if they were bad people, they were probably working out how they could cheat others out of their food," added Whitby.

"So no more expensive meals for anyone, then," said Caravan Bear.

"Or presents."

Christopher Rabbit continued. "Like everyone else in the country, the son began to get very hungry."

"Why didn't he just go home?" asked Hector.

"I don't know. Perhaps he didn't think of it."

"What did he do then?"

"He found work on a pig farm."

"Well, that was all right," said Whitby. "Pigs are OK. Except for Runt."

"It wasn't like that," said Christopher Rabbit. "In those days in the country Jesus lived in, pigs were thought of as unclean. You'd have to be desperate to get a job looking after them. But the son was desperate. He was starving. So he worked on the farm and found that even the pigs were fed better than he was. He grew more and more hungry and more and more unhappy."

"So why didn't he go home?" Hector asked again.

"Perhaps he was ashamed to," said Caravan Bear. "Would you want to go home after having spent all your father's money?"

"You mean he thought his father would say that it was his own fault and wouldn't take him back?" asked Whitby.

"I expect so."

"He stayed working on the pig farm until he couldn't bear it any longer. 'My father's servants are fed better than I am, so I'll ask him if I can come back to the farm as one of his servants,' he thought. So he left the farm and started to make the long journey home."

"How did he eat?" asked Hector.

"Maybe he did odd jobs," said Caravan Bear. "Or

ate fruit and things from the trees and bushes."

"I bet he was scared as he got closer to home," said Whitby.

"Why?"

"He probably thought his father would tell him off."

"Or beat him," said Hector.

"Or both," said Whitby cheerfully.

"Would you do that if you'd been his father?" asked Christopher Rabbit.

While the animals were thinking about it, Christopher Rabbit went on. "He was still some way from home when he saw his father in the distance running to meet him…"

"With a big stick?" asked Whitby.

"No. When his father reached him, he threw his arms around him, gave him a big hug, and kissed him."

"That was nice of him," said Caravan Bear.

"His son said, 'Father, I've done bad things and I'm not worthy to be your son. Just treat me as one of your servants.' But his father didn't do that. Instead he called his servants and told them to bring the best clothes for his son and prepare a great feast."

"And is that the end of the story?" asked Whitby.

"No," said Christopher Rabbit. "There's a bit more yet. You've forgotten the farmer's other son. The one who stayed behind."

"Did he come running with a big stick?" asked Whitby.

"Not quite. When he heard all the commotion, he came running from the field where he'd been working – and when he saw his brother, he was furious.

"'Look!' he said to his father, 'All these years I've slaved away on the farm, done everything you asked me, never even thought of going away. But you never made a feast for me, did you? You never gave me the best clothes!

"'Then my brother comes home after leaving you. He comes home ragged and starving having spent all your money, and what do you do? You give him the best clothes and make a great feast for him! It's not fair! It's just not fair!'"

"He's got a point," said Whitby.

"I agree," said Hector.

"Well, I don't know," said Christopher Rabbit. "I mean, if I'd been the father, I think I'd have been pleased to see my son again."

"That's because you're a nice rabbit," said Whitby. "I'm not."

"You're not a rabbit, you're a dog."

"You know what I mean."

"But it wasn't really fair, was it?" said Hector.

"What did his father say to the other son? The one who stayed behind?" asked Caravan Bear.

"He said, 'Look, son, you're always with me and you'll have everything that's mine when I'm dead. But this is your brother. It was as if he had died and has now come back to life. He was lost and now he's found.'"

"Hmm," said Whitby. "I'm still not convinced."

"Look at it another way," said Christopher Rabbit. "I think what Jesus was saying is that everyone, no matter what they've done, no matter how bad they've been, no matter how far they've gone away from God, is welcomed back home to him."

The animals thought about it for a moment. "That's different," Whitby said at last. "I still think it was a bit hard on the other son, though."

"But the other son didn't need to be forgiven," said Caravan Bear. "He must have known that his father loved him."

"Nice to be told though, once in a while," said Whitby stubbornly.

They had been sitting in the caravan while Christopher Rabbit was telling them the story – apart from Hector, who was outside but had his head through the window. Suddenly there was a loud banging on the door. It was the park-keeper.

"You can't stay here!" he said. "I'm just about to lock the gates so I'll thank you to take your contraption out of this car park."

"Can't we stay just for the night?" asked Caravan Bear.

"No," said the man. "It's against the rules."

So Caravan Bear, Whitby, Hector, and Christopher Rabbit got ready to leave, watched all the time by the park-keeper, who tut-tutted and kept looking at his watch as if to say that they were taking a long time.

They drove out of the park and out of the town, and it was quite late when they stopped in a lay-by beside the road.

"It was a good story," said Caravan Bear.

"I wish the park-keeper had been like the father in the story," said Whitby.

"What, welcomed us, told us to stay, and given us a feast?" laughed Caravan Bear. He turned out the lights.

Christopher Rabbit put away his Bible. "Thank you, Jesus, for the story of the lost son," he said.

"I'm glad God cares for all of us and not just the good ones," Whitby added. "Otherwise I'd have no chance."

Then they all went to sleep.

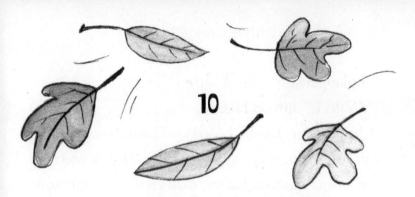

10

The Three Servants

The weather was turning colder and the days were getting shorter: winter was approaching. The holiday was coming to an end and everyone felt sad.

"I know," said Caravan Bear as they neared Christopher Rabbit's home, "we'll park in the woods behind your burrow and hold a coming-home party for your friends and neighbours."

"Really?" asked Christopher Rabbit. "That's very nice of you."

"What's nice about it?" asked Whitby.

"Saying you'll hold a party for my friends and neighbours," said Christopher Rabbit.

"Nothing nice about it," said Caravan Bear. "Last time you came home your friends and neighbours gave you a party, so we'll do the same for them."

"I like parties," said Whitby.

"So do I," agreed Hector.

Christopher Rabbit, Caravan Bear, and Whitby spent some time making preparations. There was a lot to be done. Hector, having delivered the invitations written by Christopher Rabbit, soon felt that he had done enough and took himself off to a nice quiet spot nearby.

As dusk began to fall, Caravan Bear lit lanterns in the caravan and hung them on the trees surrounding the glade in which the caravan was parked.

Soon Christopher Rabbit's friends began to arrive.

Min the cat came first, carrying a bag of knitting. Min liked to knit. Then Henry the beaver turned up with his family – they were all plastered with mud as they'd been damming a nearby stream.

"We won't come inside, thank you," said Henry. "We're a bit grubby."

Susie the squirrel was next. She brought a bag of nuts to add to the feast.

Frank the mole burrowed in, and then Lantwit the owl flew down and landed on the roof of the caravan. A passing party of mice sniffed the air and wondered whether to join the party, although they'd

not been invited, but when they saw Lantwit, they hurried away.

It was a good party. Some time later, when everyone had eaten and drunk as much as they wanted, Whitby said, "Tell us a story, Christopher Rabbit."

"Yes, tell us a story," chorused the others, so Christopher Rabbit went into the caravan – it was a fine night and they were all sitting outside – and returned carrying his Bible.

"What sort of story would you like?" he asked.

"A happy story," said Hector.

"A sad story," said Susie, cracking a nut in her paws.

"An interesting story," said Min, finishing off a row of knitting.

"I don't like scary stories," said Whitby.

"A story that makes us think," said Lantwit.

"But not too much," said Hector. "I'm not that good at thinking."

Christopher Rabbit blinked. How was he to please everyone?

"Tell us one of Jesus' stories," said Caravan Bear.

"All right." Christopher Rabbit turned the pages. "I'll tell you the story of the three servants. A rich man was getting ready to go away for a long time. He called his servants and told them he was giving them his money to look after while he was gone."

"That wasn't a very good idea," said Henry the beaver. "I wouldn't trust even my own sons with my money if I were going away."

"Oh, Dad!" said one of his sons.

"Not that you have any money anyway," said his wife.

"That's true."

Christopher Rabbit went on. "He gave five bags of gold to one servant, two bags to another, and one bag to the third."

"Why didn't he give each of them… let's see… five and two and one makes…" Whitby stopped.

"Eight," said Lantwit. "I'm quite good at adding up," he added.

"So why didn't he give each servant…" Whitby stopped once more.

"Three into eight doesn't go," said Lantwit.

"This is all getting a bit boring," said Min, reaching for another ball of wool. "Can we get on with the story, please?"

"He probably gave the most important servant five bags, then the next important two bags and the least important just one bag," said Hector. "Simple really."

"Anyway, he gave them the money and set off on his trip," Christopher Rabbit went on. "The first servant, the one who'd been given five bags of gold, invested the money and earned five more bags of gold. The servant who'd been given two bags of gold also managed to earn two more. But the servant who only received one bag dug a hole in the ground and hid the money."

"Very wise," said Frank the mole. "Everything's safer underground."

"When I collect nuts in the autumn to keep me from being hungry in the winter, I hide them in a safe place," said Susie the squirrel.

"Where?" asked Whitby.

"It wouldn't be safe if I told you."

"I wouldn't want to steal your nuts!" said Whitby. "I just like being told secrets."

"If I told you, it wouldn't be a secret any more," Susie replied.

"I suppose not."

"If you've both quite finished, perhaps Christopher Rabbit could get on with the story," said Min. Whitby and Susie said they were sorry.

"After a long time, the man returned from his trip."

"I hope he had a good holiday," said Caravan Bear. "Everyone needs holidays."

"It might not have been a holiday," said Hector. "He might have gone on a business trip."

"Wherever it was, when he came back he called his servants and asked them to tell him how they'd used his money," said Christopher Rabbit.

"I suppose he was lucky they hadn't stolen it," said Henry. "I wouldn't have trusted them in the first place."

"The servant who had been trusted with five bags of gold…"

"… the chief servant…" Whitby added.

"… gave his master ten bags of gold. He told him, 'You gave me five bags to invest and I've earned five more.'"

"I bet he was pleased with himself," said Hector.

"Hold on a minute," said Min, holding up her paw. "I thought you said that the man had given his servants the money to keep safe, not to invest."

"Gambling," snorted Henry disapprovingly. "I don't agree with gambling."

"I don't know about that," said Christopher Rabbit. "The story says that the man was very pleased with his servant. 'Well done, you good and faithful servant!' he said to him. 'We'll have a celebration!'

"Then the servant who had been trusted with two bags of gold came forward. 'Master,' he said, 'you gave me two bags of silver and I've earned two more.'

"His master was pleased with him, too. 'Well done,' he said, 'my good and faithful servant. You've been faithful to me in handling this small amount of money, so, as a reward, I'll give you more responsibilities in future.'"

"More pay too, I hope," said Henry.

"Then the servant who'd been given one bag of gold came forward. 'Master,' he said, 'I know you're a strict man, making us servants work very hard for you. I was afraid I'd lose your money if I invested it, so I hid it. Look, here it is.' And he handed over the one sack."

"I expect it was muddy after being buried in the ground," said Frank.

"Well, that was all right, wasn't it?" asked Whitby. "The man, who I'm not sure I like, went off, leaving a total of..."

"... eight bags of gold..." said Lantwit in a bored voice.

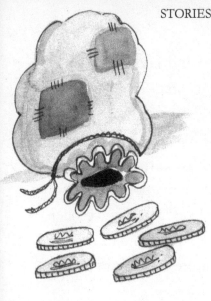

"... eight bags with his servants. He comes back to find they'd been increased by another..."

"... seven bags..." said Lantwit.

"... seven bags. So he should be delighted, even if the third servant didn't try and make any money from his bag of gold."

"He wasn't delighted," said Christopher Rabbit. "He was furious. 'You lazy and wicked servant!' he shouted. 'Why didn't you deposit my money in the bank? At least I'd have had some interest on it!'

"He ordered the bag of gold to be given to the servant who'd made the most money. And then he said that those who use what they've been given will be given more – but those who do nothing with what they've been given will have whatever they started with taken away. He ordered the other servants to throw the third servant into prison."

"And that's it?" asked Whitby.

"That's it," said Christopher Rabbit.

Everyone was silent for a moment, thinking about it.

"It doesn't seem right, does it?" said Hector at last.

"Well no, not on the face of it," said Christopher Rabbit slowly. "But I think Jesus was saying something very different in this story."

"Different from what?" asked Hector. "I mean, there you have a man who goes off, leaving his money in the care of his servants. Two of them invested the money…"

"Gambling," said Henry.

"… and doubled the amount left to him. The third servant just kept the money safe and did nothing with it. Have I got that right?"

"Yes," said Christopher Rabbit.

"And he's the one who gets told off. So was Jesus saying that it was right to take risks and gamble with money that doesn't belong to you?" asked Hector.

"I don't think so," said Caravan Bear. "I've a feeling there's more to this story than that."

"I think so too," said Christopher Rabbit. "Look at it this way. Jesus was trying to tell his listeners about God and about us, wasn't he? So let's think of the bags of money as things that we're good at. Gifts and abilities that God has given us. If we don't do anything with these gifts then it's a waste. A waste for us and a waste for all the good we can do and God can do through us. We've all got special things that God has given to us and to no one else. It's how we use them that matters."

The animals thought about this.

"I'm good at damming streams," said Henry proudly. "And I'm bringing up my boys to be good at it too."

"I'm good at searching for nuts," said Susie, "but that's only because I'd be hungry if I didn't. Mind you, I have got a large family to feed so it's just as well I'm good at it."

"I'm good at catching mice," said Lantwit.

"Just as well there aren't any here tonight, then," said Whitby. "What are you good at, Min?"

"I'm good at knitting..." Min began.

"And being a good neighbour," Christopher

Rabbit went on.

"And being nosy," said Frank, but he said it quietly and no one heard him.

"I'm good at towing the caravan," said Hector.

"Apart from the times you go too fast," said Whitby. "To say nothing about the times you get us stuck in holes in the road."

"*You* try towing, then," said Hector placidly. "What gifts has God given you, then, Whitby?

"I don't know."

"Shepherding sheep?"

"That's not fair and I said I was sorry," Whitby said angrily.

"You're funny, Whitby," said Caravan Bear. "You make us all laugh. That's important."

"Well, you keep the caravan nice," Whitby replied to him. "And you look after us all."

"And Christopher Rabbit reads us all these wonderful stories from the Bible that tell us more about God and make us think."

"Only because I was given a present of a Bible," said Christopher Rabbit.

"So if that's what the story is really about, it's how we use the gifts God has given us that's important," said Caravan Bear thoughtfully.

"And whether we bother to find out what they are and use them at all," said Lantwit. "Well, it's been a lovely evening and I'm now going to use the gift God has given me to hunt for some mice. Thank you for inviting me."

With that she hooted twice, flapped her wings, and flew off.

"When are you off again, Christopher Rabbit?" Min asked, tucking away her knitting needles.

Christopher Rabbit looked at his three friends and didn't answer. They might not want to take him away with them next time. Caravan Bear realized what he was thinking and gave him a smile.

"When the weather gets warmer," he said, "we'll all be off on our travels."

"Where will you go?" asked Min, who liked to know what was going on.

"Oh, here…" Caravan Bear began.

"And there…" said Hector.

"Wherever the fancy takes us," finished Christopher Rabbit and Whitby.

"Well, it'll be nice having you around for a while, Christopher Rabbit," Min smiled.

One by one Christopher Rabbit's friends and neighbours left, and soon only Caravan Bear, Whitby, Hector, and Christopher Rabbit remained in the glade in the wood surrounded by the food left over from the party.

"I'm tired," said Caravan Bear. "Let's leave clearing up until the morning."

"I'll blow out the candles if you like," Christopher Rabbit offered.

Caravan Bear and Whitby disappeared into the caravan, Hector made his way across the glade, and Christopher Rabbit walked around, blowing out the candles in the lanterns. Once he had blown out the last one, he stopped for a moment.

"Thank you, God, for giving each one of us some special gift. Help us to know what it is and use it to help others. And thank you, Jesus, for telling us all these important stories to help us live well."

He looked around. The glade and the surrounding wood were in darkness. The only light came from the caravan, where Caravan Bear had left a lantern glowing so that Christopher Rabbit could see his way back.

"I'll go home tomorrow," he thought. "Tonight I'll

stay in the caravan." He looked up at the black night sky, scattered with twinkling white stars. "Thank you, God, for a lovely holiday. And thank you for all my friends."

Christopher Rabbit felt very happy and contented as he crossed the glade, walked up the steps, blew out the lantern, and went to bed.

Other titles by Avril Rowlands

The Animals' Caravan

The Journey Begins

Avril Rowlands

Adventures through the Bible with Caravan Bear and friends

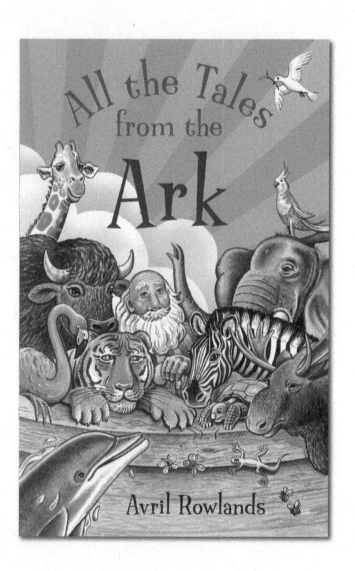

All the Tales
from the
Ark

Avril Rowlands